OF STONE AND ROPE

POEMS

DARIUS AJAI FRASURE

ASSURE PRESS

Copyright © 2019 by **Darius Ajai Frasure**

All rights reserved. No part of this book may be performed, recorded, used or reproduced in any manner whatsoever without the written consent of the author and the permission of the publisher except in the case of brief quotations embodied in critical articles and review.

An imprint of Assure Press Publishing & Consulting, LLC

www.assurepress.org

ASSURE PRESS

Publisher's Note: Assure Press books may be purchased for educational, business, or sales promotional use. For information please visit the website.

of stone and rope/ Darius Ajai Frasure. -- 1st ed.
ISBN-13: 978-1-7335897-0-3
eISBN-13: 978-1-7335897-1-0

and Joshua said unto them... take you up every man of you a stone upon his shoulder... and these stones shall be for a memorial unto the children of Israel forever.

-Joshua 4:5 KJV

Jump rope chants provided oral lessons and warnings of the potential difficulties of life... early academic instruction... opportunities to experiment with the rhythm of the language. The words and beat of a jump rope chant demand involvement, participation, and action while simultaneously offering generational connection, encouragement, and verbal challenge.

-Ming Fang, "Personal, Passionate, Participatory Inquiry: Research for the Social Justice"

OF STONE AND ROPE

I

vessels of memory package times past
concrete bridges between substance and sorrow
yesterday and tomorrow's shadow

though the present not as bright
as living in reflection of ancestors
great aunts cousins and uncles

now muted
brothers and silent
sisters

I I

without a symbol for an anchor we
    bask in allusions like

          down by the riverside
          down by the riverside
          I'm gonna lay down my burdens

III

some thought we
crossed over like
the children of Jehovah

with our contributions
fermented culture

rock blues hip-hop
Jordan Iverson Pac
Big NWA 50 Cent
Beyoncé OutKast

and *everybody loves Kanye*
like Kanye
loves Kanye

M.L.K.
that's what that day
means right?

IV

but standing on their shoulders
Phyllis Paul Langston

and their shoulders
Harriet Frederick Marcus
W.E.B.

and their shoulders
four little girls

and their shoulders
Linda Medgar Malcolm
Martin Fred Stokely

like the children of Moses
carrying those boulders

we also stack stones
as tribute

V

instruments become monuments
carry our story our culture
our new oral tradition

like skipping—no—that's white—like jump-rope in neighborhood
streets—none of this means the land is dry

we still wet
and the ground isn't fertile yet

VI

truth
just a few yards
distant

the tree
roots underground
before it owns
the surface

VII

clenching low
    hanging
   fruit

Barack Obama

I still see strange fruit
    ripened from
   trauma

VIII

America can't dangle a black man
and expect that I not be traumatized
the image is burned into me

IX

we share the tears of natives
though our trail was different

nobody has a settlement
in the land of entitlement

there is no memorial in D.C.
that can bring justice to these

bastards of dreams

the afterbirth of a nation

X

we sing rap dance and shout out blues
rock and roll these stones to have a place
we can call home away
from home

we are alone

XI

wailing widows and orphans
transported through time
by navy of corpses

husbands fathers sons

sailing blood oceans that ruin concrete
thick and hard as the bars on a cell block

holding hopes of those too dark to sell rock
without consequence

shackling bodies too colored to sell trees
without harsher sentence

XII

American justice
systemic standards
deviate by degrees
too close to see

a fly on a portrait
an intimate tapestry

XIII

so colored is the backdrop

if you're *coloured* then you're black
an afterthought of progress
because now somehow

all lives matter

even though
I thought *we had next*

XIV

it's amazing
little girls play jump rope
when their daddies used to swing
from the throat

from neck to feet
through spirit and song

both ways our story is told

XV

we are yet a broken people

that's why our poets don't recite lines
they spit pieces

and you can't hear their words
you've got to feel them

MIDDLE PASSAGE OF HOPE

- I

come by here my Lord
come by here

In 1926 Carter G. Woodson
established negro history week

it blossomed into a month

just 28 days plus one
when the year leap minus
Juneteenth

but for the African American
this is more than just *his* story

- I I

beaten bound gagged
defeated found dragged

across nations
plantations

away from familiar
faces former pharaohs
priests collected greatness

manifest destination

- I I I

western European invasion
colonization

sailing across oceans seven
oceans six oceans five
generations past

black forefathers of young
men now not meant to see 21

-IV

invaluable cargo
shipped steerage
stuffed like other means

for sharks to feed and
wonder why some believe
this very spot in the ocean
still fertile for sharks
to breed in

- V

the deep end
    for Africans who couldn't make it over
    over the side

limbs lives linked chained
    human anchors sinking to meet their fate

but for those still on the ship
this was just the beginning of the trade

for textiles common goods
rum cotton tobacco sugar cane

and black skin
the oil of that day

-VI

slave ships shipped slaves west

brought to build what pride lust greed
envy sloth wrath and gluttony started
capitalism sparked it

reach for the stars kid
but only if you're white
wealthy and male
yeah this is *his* story

-VII

it's not hard to see why most Afrocentric
ideals appear partially Marxist

it does *take a village to raise a child*
but it also takes a child's faith to truly see

-VIII

black women bear community
balance churches with babies
strapped to backs
feed black men

orphans who sag pants to their knees
brainwashed livestock promiscuous breeders
searching for the remaining 2/5ths of manhood
behind Eve's leaves

- I X

young men made into trees
without roots that only uproot
plants to smoke weed and drink
to ease their bruised
mentality emotionally scarred
spiritually confused

-x

anger spawns
regenerates
black holocaust

cycle of brutality
generational curses define
dysfunctional family

Lord come by here

-XI

the hangman's noose tightens its grip
    willie lynch—
       less fable than saint nick

more so-called reality shows
gold and platinum chains for industrial
slaves still holding to the Christ
crucified blinding eyes
the reason our youth are losing their lives
holding *heat* and living for *ice*

    the shackles we now wear are watches
    stop watch and you'll see

-XII

listen to their rhymes observe the times
massa's whip still lashes our backs
pushing *phat* whips through the 'hood
bubbling crack *busting gats* and seven
eight and nine-year-old babies
going crazy running around elementary
schools *strapped*

Lord come by here

-XIII

scarecrows and jim
crow for scared coons
nothing more than sambos
aunt jemimas and buffoons

the sharecropper's system
still keep us from going north
growing up like Harlem
New York

listen

poetry speaks

-XIV

the renaissance can happen again

in the spirit of our ancestors

    Louis Armstrong Duke Ellington Countee Cullen Aaron
    Douglas Lena Horne Dorthy West

    try Langston Hughes for the blues
    or the soul of Paul Laurence Dunbar

- X V

and the residue levied by hurricane
Katrina is still so devastating
so is the fate of so many Haitians
Texans Puerto Ricans

but legislation like *no child left behind*
holds most teachers in naturally
heterogeneous classrooms just
babysitting the death of this nation

forced to cut some slack to the slackers
something's up with that

-XVI

standardized tests
just hold us back
first grade and we're ahead
but by third we're beaten back

who is it that's been *left behind*

it ain't hard to tell

-XVII

but we always hope
black president
2009
number 44

12 years after Biggie'
13 after 'Pac
44 after Malcolm
45 after Martin

barely a few generations past
marching in the heat
of the movement

-XVIII

at first it seemed our legacy
in this country would only be
death chains and knees

but black folks just *keep hope alive*
and dreamers still dream
on their feet

every day

ABOUT THE AUTHOR

Professor Darius Frasure is a highly sought after educator, poet, mentor, coach, and consultant. He holds degrees from Paul Quinn College, Luther Rice Seminary, National University, and Fielding Graduate University. His work revolves around partnerships with literary arts and education organizations. His writing appears in many literary journals, and select readings are on youtube. He has one spoken word album, Spoken Pieces (2010), and two collections of poetry: stained glass medusa (2015) and of stone and rope (2019).

    Contact and booking: dariusfrasure.com

- goodreads.com/dariusfrasure
- linkedin.com/in/dariusfrasure
- twitter.com/dariusfrasure
- facebook.com/dariusfrasure
- instagram.com/dariusfrasure

www.ingramcontent.com/pod-product-compliance
Lightning Source LLC
Chambersburg PA
CBHW060508080526
44584CB00015B/1595